Victorian Britain

Tony D. Triggs

This book is dedicated to Heather

ACKNOWLEDGEMENTS

The author and publisher would like to thank the following for permission to reproduce photographs and other material:

Aerofilms Limited	5
Architectural Association	38; 39
Barnardo Photo Library	10
Beamish, The North Of England Open Air Museum	13; 32; 42-43; 47
By permission of the British Library	27
ET Archive	40
Hulton-Deutsch Collection	cover; 6; 8; 11; 19; 34-35; 46
Humberside County Libraries	13
The Illustrated London News Picture Library	35
The IronBridge Gorge Museum	21
Leicestershire Museums (Newton Collection)	15
Mansell Collection	5; 6; 8; 10; 12; 14; 22; 24; 29; 31; 36-37; 39; 44
Mary Evans Picture Library	7; 9; 12; 15; 16; 17; 18; 19; 20; 22; 23; 28; 37; 41; 45
Bradford Metropolitan Libraries	33
National Portrait Gallery	4; 29
Reproduced by permission of the National Postal Museum	13
By permission of the National Railway Museum, York	16; 17
Punch	26
University Library, Keele	25
Wood Visual Communications	30-31
National Coal Mining Museum for England	21

First published 1992 by Folens Limited. Revised edition published 1995.
United Kingdom: Folens Publishers, Apex Business Centre, Boscombe Road, Dunstable, LU5 4RL.
Email: folens@folens.com

Ireland: Folens Publishers, Greenhills Road, Tallaght, Dublin 24.
Email: info@folens.ie

Poland: JUKA, ul. Renesansowa 38, Warsaw 01-905

This book was previously published as *Primary History: Victorian Britain*.

Cover design: Design for Marketing, Ware

Every effort has been made to contact copyright holders of material used in this book. If any have been overlooked, we will be pleased to make any necessary arrangements.

British Library Cataloguing in Publication Data. A catalogue record for this book is available from the British Library.

Tony D Triggs hereby asserts his moral rights to be identified as the author of this work in accordance with the Copyright, Designs and Patents Act 1988.

ISBN 1 85276 823-1

CONTENTS

1. The Victorian Age

From 1837 to 1901 Great Britain had a queen called Queen Victoria. In those days Britain was very powerful, and it ruled many overseas countries including Canada and parts of Africa. These countries made up the British Empire, and Victoria was their queen too.

Britain was the world's greatest shipbuilding country; its navy helped to keep control of overseas countries and its cargo boats brought their cotton, rubber, metal and other products to Britain. British factories turned these products into finished goods. For example, the cotton was turned into cloth for making clothes. Then the goods were sold at a profit. Factory owners grew very rich but their workers were often badly paid, especially at the start of Victoria's reign.

There were many important changes during Victoria's reign. In 1837 most people lived in villages and worked on the land; by 1901 many had moved into towns to find work in factories, shops and offices. The growth of towns went on throughout Queen Victoria's reign, and so did the efforts to stop them getting too filthy and crowded.

? A time of change

The two drawings below show Swindon (a town in Wiltshire) at the start and end of Victoria's reign.

1. Which drawing is the earlier one? Why do you think so? List some of the changes which you can see. What things are the same? What do the changes tell you about people's lives during Queen Victoria's reign?

Back-to-back Victorian housing.

In a time of change the Queen was a very important figure. She stood for things that mattered to people; for example, she made them feel proud to be British, and they admired her respectable family life. In 1887 and 1897 there were huge Jubilee (or anniversary) celebrations to mark her fiftieth and sixtieth years as Queen.

 Is there a Jubilee Street near you?

Some towns have streets called Jubilee Street.

1. When do you think these streets were built?
2. See if your town has streets named after Queen Victoria, her husband Albert or the Jubilees. (A street map may help you.)
3. Try to check when the houses were built. (One of them may have a special stone which gives the date.)

This book is about life in Britain during Victoria's reign. This period (1837-1901) is sometimes called the Victorian Age.

 Victorian children - rich and poor

Look at the pictures on this page.

1. Why do you think the houses were built back-to-back?
2. How did people heat their homes?
3. Describe the activities which took place in a back yard.
4. Which children are poor and which are well off?
5. How can you tell whether the girl with the basket is poor or well off?
6. Look at the well off children's faces. What might they be thinking?

A handloom weaver's cottage.

2. The Spread of Steam Power

For hundreds of years, villagers in Britain had farmed the land with sickles and other simple tools. As well as growing food for themselves they made their own cloth by spinning and weaving the wool from their sheep or the fibres from plants. Some earned money by spinning and weaving in their homes. They did this using simple looms which they worked by hand.

The power of steam was not discovered until the end of the 17th century. The first steam engines were used to pump water out of flooded mines. Then, in the 18th century, they were sometimes used in factories to work machines.

Steam-powered machines could do spinning and weaving far quicker than they could be done by hand. Soon there was no paid work for people to do in their cottages, and countryfolk had to leave their homes and find jobs in the factories.

Mule spinning.

By the start of Queen Victoria's reign enormous factories were being built, and towns for the workers grew up near them.

More people left the countryside as steam-powered machines replaced workers on farms. Thousands of families crowded into the towns each year to find work in the factories.

The picture above shows men working on a farm. The men have a steam engine. It runs on coal and can pull heavy loads along like a tractor. (This sort of engine is sometimes called a traction engine.) This time the engine is standing still and working the other machine, which threshes corn (beats it to separate the seeds from the stalks).

Life after steam

Read this page carefully and look at the pictures.

1. Discuss with a partner how the coming of steam has changed people's lives. Copy and complete the chart.

Person	How life changed	Better or worse
Landowner		
Farmworker		
Factory owner		
Handloom weaver		
Children		

'Please, Sir, I want some more.'
'What!' said the master at length, in a faint voice.
'Please, Sir,' replied Oliver, 'I want some more.'

A workhouse yard.

3. Prison and Workhouse

Sometimes there were not enough jobs for everyone, even in towns with factories. Workers were often paid very badly, but those without work got nothing at all. Some families starved but others went to live in a workhouse.

In the workhouse people were kept alive but treated as harshly as possible. This was to make sure families would avoid going there unless they were really desperate.

Husbands, wives and children had to live apart, and no one could have any outings, visitors, tobacco or beer.

Everyone - apart from old folk and disabled people - had to do back-breaking work. For example, they had to smash rocks to pieces, ready for use in mending roads.

Men working in the workhouse.

In 1865 the *Daily Telegraph* described how a man had died at home because he could not face life in a workhouse:

He and his son used to work night and day repairing boots to try... and pay for the room ... so as to keep the home together. On Friday night, when they had not even a halfpenny to buy a candle, he got up from his bench and began to shiver. He threw down the boots, saying, "Someone else must finish these when I am gone, for I can do no more." There was no fire, and he said,"I would be better if I was warm."

His wife ... took two pairs of ... boots to sell at the shop, but she could only get [enough for] coal and a little tea and bread, and her husband died on Saturday morning. When she was asked why they did not go into the workhouse the wife replied:
"We wanted the comforts of our little home."

Someone asked what the comforts were, for he only saw a little straw in the corner of the room, the windows of which were broken. The wife began to cry, and said that they had a quilt and other little things. Once, when the man applied ... for aid, the ... officer gave him a 4lb loaf and told him that if he came again he should get the 'stones'.

The son explained why they could not spend the winter in the workhouse:
"When we came out in the summer we should be like people dropped from the sky. No one would know us, and we would not have even a room. I could work now if I had food, for my sight would get better."

 Home sweet home?

Read the description from the *Daily Telegraph* and look at the picture of men working in the workhouse.

1. What do you know about the family's food, heating, lighting and bedding?
2. What happened to the boots once the family had mended them?
3. What do you think the officer meant by the 'stones'? (Look at page 11.)
4. What were the family's reasons for avoiding the workhouse?
5. Describe the workers' seats. Why do you think they were made like this?

 Life in the workhouse

Use the extract from the *Daily Telegraph*.

1. Write a list of rules people had to obey in the workhouse. Include rules you have read about but also add some rules of your own.
2. Turn your list of rules into a notice for the classroom wall.

 Oliver Twist

The conversation at the top of page 8 comes from the novel *Oliver Twist* by Charles Dickens.

1. Where do you think it is taking place?
2. What is happening?
3. Why does Oliver have to ask twice?
   (Say what you think and then find out from the novel if necessary. The conversation takes place near the start of the novel.)

Thomas Barnado provided hostels where hundreds of homeless children could live.

Some Victorians tried to help people who were being ill-treated. At the start of Queen Victoria's reign Elizabeth Fry called for better conditions in prisons, especially for women.

Better conditions

Look at the picture below which shows Elizabeth Fry visiting a prison.

1. Try to pick out Elizabeth Fry in the painting. What do you think she is doing?
2. Fry has brought some visitors to the prison. Which are the visitors and which are the prisoners? How can you tell?
3. What happened to children if their mothers were sent to prison?
4. Does this prison seem as bad as the one Dickens describes? In what way does it seem different?
5. Fry always tried to see every part of the prisons she visited.
   Why do you think this was so important?

Breaking stones.

Writers like Dickens made sure no one forgot the cruel way many workers and prisoners were treated.

 For example, in *Pickwick Papers* he described a prison where people went if they were in debt:

Mr Tom Roker ... led the way through an iron gate.
"Oh," said Mr Pickwick, looking down a dark and filthy staircase, which appeared to lead to a row of damp and gloomy stone caverns beneath the ground ... "You don't really mean to say that human beings live down in those wretched dungeons."
"Live down there! Yes, and die down there, too, very often," replied Mr Roker; "and what of that?"

 The evidence

Think about the report in the *Daily Telegraph* and what Dickens says in the *Pickwick Papers*.

1. Which do you think gives more reliable information? Why do you think so?
2. What do you think Mr Pickwick might have replied when Mr Roker said, "and what of that?"
3. Make a list of reasons why Elizabeth Fry and Thomas Barnardo wanted to help poor people.
4. Can you think of reasons why some people objected to their actions?

4. The Railways

Until Queen Victoria's time most people spent their lives in the village where they were born. They might go to market in a neighbouring town but they rarely went further.

Some business people did make long journeys. Often they travelled in the horse-drawn stage coaches that linked London with other parts of the country.

Shorter journeys were usually made on foot or on horseback. Horses were very important indeed for transporting goods.

They pulled farm wagons along country roads and they hauled heavy barges along canals.

They also hauled wagons of coal, stone and other supplies. Often the wagons were linked together to form long trains, and the horses pulled them along special tracks. Sometimes goods were taken from barges and put into wagons to finish their journey.

The horse-drawn 'trains' developed into proper railways. Steam engines fixed at the top of a hill were sometimes used to haul wagons up by means of chains. Then people started to fix an engine at the front of a train. The engine travelled along a track and pulled the train with it.

? Stage coaches and trains

Read this page carefully and look at the pictures.

1. Who might have said the words at the start of the chapter?
2. Why do you think he said them?
3. The painting on the left was done in Queen Victoria's reign. What was the artist saying about the two forms of transport?
4. How did the invention of the railway change people's lives?
5. Did some people benefit more than others? Give reasons for your answers.

The Lady Mary.

Locomotive at Beamish Museum.

Industrial locomotives

Look at the photograph of the Lady Mary.

1. One man drove the engine and the other stoked the boiler. Describe what job each man is doing.
2. Compare the photographs of the two trains. Is the Beamish train a good reconstruction? Give reasons for your answer.
3. Why do you think museums reconstruct trains?
4. Make a list of people who might want to see and ride on old locomotives. Can you think of different reasons they might have?
5. Draw an old locomotive and find out about and label the parts.

A special year

Look at the picture of the stamp on this page.

1. The stamp appeared in 1975, 150 years after something special had happened.
   What was it?
2. Why was the event special?
3. How do you know this stamp was not produced in 1825?

New railway tracks were quickly built. One of the most important linked Stockton and Darlington in the north of England. It was opened in 1825 and some people say it was the first proper railway in the world. Not only did the trains have locomotives (engines on wheels) but anyone could use them for goods or travel (other railways were private).

Railways were soon being built throughout Britain. By the middle of Queen Victoria's reign nearly every big town and village had a station.

Stephenson's Locomotion

7ᵖ

1825 Stockton and Darlington Railway

There comes a crowd of burly navvies, with pickaxes and barrows, and ... the hills are cut through.

NAVVY IN HEAVY MARCHING ORDER.

5. Navvies at Work

Railway builders had a very hard and dangerous life. The men (called navvies) worked with spades and barrows to take away unwanted soil. Often, the men lived in camps beside new railway lines.

 A writer described the conditions at the time:

Some slept in huts constructed of damp turf, cut from the wet grass, too low to stand upright in ... Others formed a room of stones ... The rain beat through the roof, and ... the wind swept through the holes. If they caught a fever they died, or wandered in the open air, spreading the disease wherever they went. In these huts they lived with their women.

 In 1846 a railway boss described to some members of Parliament how he treated his workers.

The men live in wooden buildings, with a room for cooking and ... hammocks slung along each side.
One man's wife cooks for the whole of them?
Yes.
You do not allow any other women in the camp?
No.

 The navvy

Look at the pictures and read the description of life on the railway.

1. List the things the navvy is carrying. In each case suggest why he needed it.
2. Look at the two descriptions of the navvies' camps. Which camp seems to be better? Why?
3. Who is asking the questions in the second paragraph?
4. Do you think the navvies would have liked a chance to give their opinions too? Why?
5. Why might a navvy be afraid to complain?

Some railway workers had come from Ireland to escape from starvation. Many Irish people lived on potatoes, which they grew on their own small plots of land. In the late 1840s the potato plants were hit by disease and the crops were poor.

Some Irish people found jobs and homes in English cities. Others helped to build railways. Because they were used to a very hard life they often did the hardest, most dangerous jobs, like digging tunnels and using explosives.

 A hard and dangerous life

Think about the life of a navvy.

1. Suggest some of the dangers they faced in their work.
2. How might working conditions have been improved?
3. Why do you think such improvements were not made?

A navvies' camp. Which of the two descriptions opposite fits it better?

IN MEMORY
OF THE UNFORTUNATE MEN
WHO LOST THEIR LIVES WHILE ENGAGED IN THE CONSTRUCTION OF THE
BRAMHOPE TUNNEL OF THE LEEDS AND THIRSK RAILWAY,
FROM 1845 TO 1849.
THIS TOMB IS ERECTED AS A MEMORIAL
AT THE EXPENSE OF JAMES BRAY, ESQ., THE CONTRACTOR AND OF THE
AGENTS, SUB-CONTRACTORS AND WORKMEN EMPLOYED THERON.

"I am a Stranger and a Sojourner with you give me a possession of a Burying-Place with you, that I may bury my Dead out of my sight." "Or those Eighteen upon whom the Tower in Siloam fell and slew them; think ye that they were sinners above all the men in Jerusalem? I tell you Nay; but except ye repent, ye shall all likewise perish."

First class travel. **A**

6. The Effect of the Railways

Trains were much quicker than coaches. A train could travel from Scotland to London in one day or night; people going by coach had to sleep in different inns on the way. Shorter journeys might take half an hour by train instead of half a day by coach.

Travel became much cheaper and easier; a coach had room for ten or twelve people, a train could take hundreds.

 People had different views about the trains. One man had this to say:

Everything is near, everything is immediate - time, distance and delay are removed.

 Some people did not like the railways. This is what someone else had to say:

I detest railways. Your railway has cut through and spoiled some of the loveliest bits of scenery in the country.

Now, every fool in Buxton can be in Bakewell in half an hour, and every fool in Bakewell can be at Buxton.

Second class travel. **B**

Third class travel. **C**

First class travel?

Look at pictures **A**, **B** and **C**.

1. Describe the differences between the carriages.
2. At the start of Queen Victoria's reign someone wrote, 'Get as far from the engine as possible'. Try to think of some reasons for this.
3. Which sort of carriage do you think was nearest the engine? Which do you think was furthest from it? Say why you think so.

The poorest workers were forced to stay in their smoky cities. Better off people could live in smaller towns and travel to work; they could also go away for holidays.

BLACKPOOL

Health & Pleasure, Glorious Sea

Rail travel

Read page 16 including the introduction.

1. What effect did the train have on the journey time between Scotland and London?
2. What do you think is meant by 'Man is become a bird'?
3. Look again at what the people said about railways. What did they like and dislike about them?
4. Say what you feel about the points they made.
5. How do you and your friends think trains affected the following:
    - factory owners;
    - stage coach and canal companies and their employees;
    - towns like Swindon (look again at the pictures on pages 4 and 5);
    - seaside towns like Blackpool;
    - the range of fresh food which people ate;
    - the spread of news and ideas;
    - the very poor.

Scotland to London

According to a Victorian writer, 'The early Scotsman scratches himself in the morning mists of the north, and has his porridge in London before the setting sun'.

1. Discuss what the writer meant.
2. Describe what the poster on page 16 is advertising.
3. How might people who saw the poster respond?

In Liverpool there were 7,860 cellars ... which were dark, damp and dirty. They were home for 39,000 people.

7. Homes of the Poor

Large numbers of people moved to the towns to find work in the mills. Many mill workers lived in cramped and filthy conditions. The rows of houses were built 'back-to-back', and this meant that each house had other houses attached on three sides. Only the front of each house could have windows, and these looked out on a narrow road or alley-way.

There was usually one room upstairs and one room downstairs. A family of up to ten or twelve people might have to share this tiny home, and sometimes three or four of them had to share one bed.

 Mrs Gaskell, a Victorian writer, described a visit to such a home:

You went down into the cellar in which a family of human beings lived. It was very dark inside ... the smell was so fetid [foul] as almost to knock the two men down ... You could just see three or four little children rolling on the wet brick floor, through which the moisture of the street oozed up; the fireplace was empty and black; the wife sat on her husband's lair [bed] and cried in the dark loneliness.

Back alleys

Look at the photograph on page 18.

1. When do you think this photograph was taken?
2. Describe what you think each woman is doing.
3. Find out what the tub might have been used for.
4. Make a list of activities people might have done in 'back alleys'.
5. Describe what it would have been like at night.

Life in a cellar

The drawing on the right, done in Victorian times, shows a cellar home. Like Mrs Gaskell, the artist is trying to tell us about the lives of the poor. Use the drawing and Mrs Gaskell's description to help you answer the following questions:

1. What is the worst thing about the cellar described by Mrs Gaskell?
   What do you think has caused this problem?
2. Why do you think the fireplace is empty?
3. A lair is a place where an animal hides.
   Why do you think Mrs Gaskell chose that particular word?
4. Look at the people in the drawing and study their faces. What do you think their feelings are?
5. What are the woman and oldest child doing?
6. Do you think the woman has warm or cold water? If it is warm how did she heat it? Where do you think she got the water?

Street life

Look at the picture of the street scene.

1. What do you think the man is doing?
2. What are the people selling?
3. What does this picture tell you about family life in Victorian times?
4. Do you think the family in the centre was poor or better off? Give a reason for your answer.

Factories and railways needed machines and engines which were made of metal. To get metal, Victorian workers heated special stone (called ore) until the metal inside it melted. Then they let the metal run into moulds to harden.

 The stone was heated in giant ovens called furnaces. According to one Victorian writer:

The heat of the furnaces is terrible and the work most exhausting. The men have to wring their clothes when they get home ...

"The work affects you all over," said a worker ... "You get so cold that you shiver so you can't hold your food. The furnaces burn the insides out of you."

The man had burns all over his body.

If you didn't work you didn't eat.

8. Victorian Workers

 A working life

Read carefully the descriptions of Victorian workers on these pages.

1. Why do you think the metal workers had to wring their clothes out when they got home?
2. One particular furnace worker is mentioned. What is wrong with him?
3. What word is used for a coal miner?
4. How can you tell that the cavern where the miner is working is small?
5. Describe what the children in the drawing on this page are doing.

Working in coal mines was just as unpleasant. Workers had to go down shafts (deep holes in the ground) to get to the coal. They climbed down ladders or were lowered on ropes, and there was always the chance of a terrible fall. At the bottom, the dangers were even worse. To get to the coal, they had to go along narrow tunnels. Sometimes there was so little room that they had to crawl on their hands and knees or slide on their stomachs. In the darkness they could hear water trickling down through the rocks.

 This is how a Victorian writer described the scene which a worker would find at the end of his tunnel:

In a cavern full of floating coal dust ... glimmer three or four candles stuck in clay. One hewer, nearly naked, lying upon his back, has his small, sharp pick-axe a little above his nose and picking into the coal ...

Iron works, Coalbrookdale.

A life of danger

Using candles in a mine was especially dangerous.

1. Try to find out the reasons for this.
2. What other dangers faced Victorian miners? You can probably think of three or four by yourself (or with your friends).
3. What effects did the building of iron works have on the environment?

Ancient or modern?

Look at the small photograph below. It was taken in a modern museum and shows what conditions were like for children who worked in the mines.

1. How well do the conditions match those shown in the drawing on page 20?
2. Do you think the museum used modern books or Victorian books for its information?
3. Which would be better? Why do you think so?
4. What other sources of information might the museum have used?

The streets are every morning wet by the tears of children who are forced by the fear of the strap ... to hasten, half dressed, to the worsted mills.

9. Work for Women and Children

At the start of Queen Victoria's reign women and children had to work for long hours, even if their jobs were very tiring indeed. In mines, the women and children had to take the coal to the wagons at the surface. The drawings (found in Victorian books) show children moving through a tunnel and women and children working in mills.

A

 This is what starting work was like for a seven-year-old called Robert Blincoe:

They reached the mill at about half past five ... Blincoe smelt the fumes of the oil on the axles of 20,000 wheels and spindles.

The task first given to him was to pick up the loose cotton that fell onto the floor ... Nothing could be easier, although he was terrified by the whirling motion and noise of the machinery, and not a little affected by the dust ... Unused to the stench, he soon felt sick, and by constantly stooping, his back ached ... But he soon found that sitting down was strictly forbidden. His task-master said he must keep on his legs. He did so for six hours and a half, suffering greatly with hunger and thirst.

Blincoe had grown up by the start of Victoria's reign but children were still being treated in the same harsh way.

B

C

Victorian children

Look at the girls in the photograph.

1. What jobs do you think they do?
2. What is your evidence?

A working life

Bosses were often harsh and cruel but they allowed their workers to have a lunch break.

1. Why do you think they gave them a break?
2. Mining families often worked together. Do you think they were paid by the hour or by how much coal they produced in a day? Why do you think so?
3. Compare Robert's description of life in the mill with pictures **B** and **D**. How are they the same and how are they different?

Women and children

Read these pages and look carefully at the pictures.

1. How was the moving of coal dangerous?
2. List some of the things which made Robert Blincoe's morning unpleasant.
3. Why do you think some workers only saw daylight on Sundays?

Working in mills could be almost as hard as working in mines. It was dangerous too, for workers sometimes got caught in machines, and growing children were crippled by all the bending and standing they had to do.

People believed that Sunday was a day for resting and attending church, so nearly everyone had this day off work each week.

Many churches ran Sunday schools, and this was the only schooling many children got. However, some were so tired that they fell asleep and fell off their benches during the lessons.

D

He cried when he had to climb the dark flues ...; and when the soot got in his eyes ...; and when his master beat him ...; and when he had not enough to eat.

10. Young Chimney Sweeps

For most of Queen Victoria's reign, chimney sweeps employed young children to go up chimneys and sweep them clean. The work was very dangerous, for the soot got into children's lungs and into cuts on their arms and legs.

 An adult chimney sweep explained what life was like for a young chimney sweep.

The flesh must be hardened. This is done by rubbing it, chiefly on the elbows and knees, with the strongest brine. You must stand over them with a cane or coax them by a promise of a halfpenny if they will stand a few more rubs. At first they will come back from their work with their arms and knees streaming with blood and the knees looking as if the caps had been pulled off. Then they must be rubbed with brine again and perhaps go off to another chimney.

The best age for teaching boys is about six. But I have known at least two of my neighbours' children begin at the age of five.

Seven or eight years ago a boy was smothered (suffocated) in a chimney here. The doctor who opened his body said that they had pulled his heart and liver all over the place in dragging him down.

A law had been passed in 1840 to put a stop to the use of children, but people who broke the law were only fined a small sum, and most sweeps carried on as before. Their crimes were made public.

Societies were formed to make sure that people obeyed the law. Some of these Societies offered to sweep people's chimneys without using boys, and they produced cards and leaflets to let people know about their work. The card below was produced in part of Staffordshire called the Pottery or Potteries.

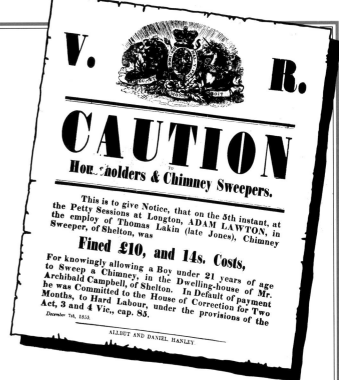

V. R.

CAUTION
Hou..holders & Chimney Sweepers.

This is to give Notice, that on the 5th instant, at the Petty Sessions at Longton, ADAM LAWTON, in the employ of Thomas Lakin (late Jones), Chimney Sweeper, of Shelton, was

Fined £10, and 14s. Costs,

For knowingly allowing a Boy under 21 years of age to Sweep a Chimney, in the Dwelling-house of Mr. Archibald Campbell, of Shelton. In Default of payment he was Committed to the House of Correction for Two Months, to Hard Labour, under the provisions of the Act, 3 and 4 Vic., cap. 85.

December 7th, 1855.

ALLBUT AND DANIEL, HANLEY.

Advertising new methods.

Public notice.

The law

Look at the public notice.

1. Why was Adam Lawton fined?
2. How much was he fined?
3. Did he pay the fine?
4. How was he punished?
5. Who do you think produced the notice? Why was it produced?

Climbing boys

Look at the boy in the picture.

1. How old do you think he is?
2. What is he holding?
3. Where is he standing?
4. What job has he done?
5. Why were small children used to sweep chimneys?

Chimney sweeps

You will need to read these pages carefully.

1. Find out what brine is. What did chimney sweeps use it for?
2. How can you tell that the brine must have hurt?
3. What were the dangers children faced when they went up chimneys?
4. What could sweeps use instead of children?
5. Why do you think people risked a fine rather than changing their methods?

> The cripples might be numbered by hundreds, perhaps by thousands ... They seemed to me, such were their crooked shapes, like a mass of crooked alphabets (letters).

THE "SILENT HIGHWAY"-MAN.

11.
Better Conditions for Workers

Some people cared very deeply about how workers were treated. One of these people was Lord Ashley, who later became the Earl of Shaftesbury.

Shaftesbury and others called for changes to stop children being worn out and crippled by their work. In 1833 (four years before the start of Queen Victoria's reign) Parliament passed a Factory Bill. It banned the use of children under nine in mills and it put a limit on older children's working hours. However, the hours were still very long, and adults were not protected at all. In any case, some employers simply ignored the new laws.

In 1842, Parliament banned the use of women, girls and young boys in coal mines. Then, in 1844 and 1847, it cut the number of hours that women and children could work in mills. Children from nine to thirteen could work for up to six and a half hours a day, and women and older children could work for up to ten hours a day.

Parliament placed a limit on the workers' hours. It tried to see that younger children had some part time schooling, and schools were often set up at factories. Finally, in 1875, Parliament made a tough new law that stopped the use of climbing boys. Inspectors checked that bosses were obeying all the new laws.

At the start of Queen Victoria's reign very few homes had their own water supply. Many homes did not have toilets, and slops were poured into the gutters. Other homes had toilets outside which did not flush and the filth went into a hole in the ground. It even got into the water used for drinking and washing, which came out of wells and public taps. Sometimes the water looked and smelled dirty; but even when it seemed to be clean it was full of germs; and deadly diseases such as typhoid spread through many cities. In the centre of Manchester most people died before they were twenty.

Early in Queen Victoria's reign a man called Edwin Chadwick said that every home should have its own toilet linked to a sewer. He also said that every home should have clean running water. By 1901, flush toilets, sewers and running water were provided in many homes. As a result, there was far less disease.

? Health conditions

Read these pages carefully and look at the map.

1. In which areas were the homes most overcrowded?
2. Which classes of people lived in the unhealthiest places? Explain your answer.
3. The cartoon at the top of page 26 was drawn in Queen Victoria's reign. What do you think the artist was trying to say?

Key

■	Houses of the working classes
▨	Shops, warehouses and houses of tradespeople
□	Houses of the upper class

Ward	Population	Population of each acre
Nos I & II	28,775	207
III, IV & V	23,039	118
VI, VII & VIII	30,306	84

Map from Chadwick's book **The Sanitary Condition of The Labouring Population of Great Britain.**

A patient inhaling chloroform. What will it do to him?

Medical treatment also improved during Victorian times. At the start of Queen Victoria's reign it was hard to carry out operations because doctors had no reliable way of easing pain, and a team of men had to hold the screaming patient down. Surgeons had to be very quick, and could only do simple operations like cutting off legs. They could not do any delicate work inside patients' bodies. During the 1840s the problem was solved by the use of anaesthetics (drugs such as ether and chloroform, which deadened pain).

Surgeons using chloroform could do all sorts of new operations, but some patients died because germs got into their wounds. Doctors were only beginning to understand about germs, but a Scottish surgeon called Joseph Lister began to use an antiseptic (or germ-killing) spray during operations. Later, he and other surgeons simply kept themselves, their tools and their hospitals as clean and germ-free as possible.

Thanks to Chadwick's ideas, Victorian people began to live longer and healthier lives. And if they did fall ill they could often be treated and cured.

Using an antiseptic spray for an operation.

An English nurse called Florence Nightingale went to the Crimea (southern Russia) to tend soldiers wounded in battle there. She helped to spread the idea that nurses and hospitals should be clean.

The drawing on the left includes two pictures of Florence Nightingale's face. What was the artist trying to say about her?

Florence Nightingale, at Scutari.

Some Victorians felt it was wrong to use anaesthetics, especially for easing the pain of childbirth. They pointed out a Bible verse that seemed to say that giving birth was meant to be painful. However, in 1857 Queen Victoria used chloroform herself.

 Improvements in medicine

Look at the painting.

1. Describe what has happened in the painting.
2. What effect do you think Queen Victoria's action had on other people?
3. What message was the artist trying to convey?

12. Saltaire Village

There were many mill owners who treated their workers cruelly, but others tried to meet their needs and give them homes that were fit to live in.

One man who treated his workers well was Sir Titus Salt. In the 1850s he built his own spinning and weaving mills, along with a village to house the workers.

Salt made sure that everything was clean and healthy. He chose a site in the Yorkshire countryside, well away from the smoke and filth of the nearest cities (Leeds and Bradford). Because the village was totally new it needed a name, and Salt decided to call it Saltaire (made up from his own name and that of the nearby River Aire).

There were no oozing gutters outside the doors, for every house had a toilet linked to underground drains.

There was water on tap, and every home had gas lamps, at least in the downstairs rooms. There were lots of large windows to let in plenty of daylight and air, and some houses even had their own gardens. Workers rented the houses for 1 shilling (5p) a week!

Most of the houses in Salt's village had two rooms downstairs and two rooms upstairs. The rooms were small but at least there was no need for parents and children to share a bed.

The village included a church, a park and a library for the workers to use.

D   E

5

4

3

2

1

D   E

Saltaire

Look at the photograph of Saltaire from the air. It will help you to answer the following questions.

1. Was the photograph taken in Salt's time or ours? How do you know?
2. Do you think all the houses shown in the photograph were built by Salt?
3. Try to pick out some of the housing built in Salt's time. Use the grid to help you.
4. Can you find Salt's mill?

Now look at the photograph at the bottom of the page. It shows Saltaire shortly after it was built.

5. Suggest some of the ways in which goods and people travelled to and from the village.
6. The village had no public house. Why do you think this was?
7. At the end of some blocks of houses there were larger houses. Suggest which workers might have lived there.
8. One house had a tower where someone could keep an eye on the villagers. How do you think they felt about being watched in this way?

When do you think this drawing was done - in Salt's time or ours? Why?

The rich man in his
    castle,
The poor man at his
    gate,
God made them, high or
    lowly,
And ordered their estate.

13. Masters and Servants

The words at the top of the page come from a hymn called 'All Things Bright and Beautiful'. Hymns like this encouraged the poor to accept their hard lives while rich folk lived in luxury. Salt's workers had homes with only two rooms, but a nearby mansion called Milner Field had over 50 rooms. There was a billiard room, a library and a music room with a huge organ. There was also a giant conservatory with marble statues and tropical plants. Every room was as comfortable and fine as possible, with beautiful carpets and chandeliers. The mansion was owned by Titus Salt (Sir Titus Salt's son).

Salt had a horse-drawn coach to take him wherever he wanted. To reach the mill he travelled down a tree-lined drive and across his own bridge. Salt and his family had over a dozen maids and servants. They treated them well but they had to work hard.

Many Victorian girls became maids, though few worked in mansions like Milner Field. Some worked in farm-houses; others found jobs in the homes of well-paid workers like bank managers. They had to sleep in the cellar or attic, and often they shared it with other maids and perhaps a number of mice or rats.

Maids were paid just a few pence a week but they got enough food to keep them alive. It was usually better to become a maid than to stay at home in a filthy slum.

Maids had to do all sorts of housework, and in those days it was harder than it is today. For example, there were no washing machines, and maids scrubbed clothes on a scrubbing board or put them in a tub and beat them with a stick called a 'dolly'.

Often, there was a housekeeper telling the maids what to do - and boxing their ears if they did it wrong.

Victorian servants

Look at the photograph on page 32.

1. Try to find out what each of these items was called.
2. Why do you think the 'dollies' have slots at the bottom?
3. Think about Salt's life and his home and list some of the things his maids and servants might have had to do.
4. What other servants might Titus Salt have employed to work at Milner Field mansion?

Rich and poor

The conditions in which people lived varied enormously.

1. Discuss why the verse at the start of this chapter is usually missed out when people sing the hymn today.
2. What is the artist trying to say about how rich and poor people lived in the drawing above?

Milner Field mansion.

I never went to school.
I got no clothes to go in.
I cannot read or write.
I don't know what you
mean by God.

14.
Schools

At the start of Queen Victoria's reign few children went to school, and they grew up unable to read or write. Church registers (records) of marriages show that only half of the people who married could sign their names.

The government did not run any schools. Some people ran small schools in their homes. Larger schools, called charity schools, were built and run by wealthy people who wanted children to learn about God and Jesus Christ.

Most charity schools had a single class and just one teacher, who taught the pupils how to read the Bible and Prayer Book. She also taught them writing, arithmetic, and perhaps some skills like sewing and gardening.

Charity schools for the very poor were called 'ragged schools'. One man explained:

When we first opened the school no less than five boys came absolutely naked except for their mothers' shawls which were pinned around them. Five separate gangs of thieves attended the school.

Schools often charged a few pence a week, and many parents could not afford it; others needed the money their children could earn at work. Because of this, most children left before they were ten. The man who founded the ragged school said that the thieves were 'all, within six months, earning their [livings] more or less respectably'. For some children, work and school went together. Children in textile (cloth) mills often worked in the morning and studied in the afternoon. Some bosses even provided a school-room at the mill.

Do the children in this classroom all look fit and well?

Girls and boys were often taught separately.

What do you think might be wrong with some of them?

 In 1843, Charles Dickens said the following about a ragool school at Field Lane in London:

It was held in a low-roofed den in a sickening atmosphere in the midst of ... dirt and disease ... The pupils ... sang, fought, danced, robbed each other - seemed possessed by legions of devils.

A few years later he said it was:

Quiet and orderly ... well white-washed, numerously attended, and thoroughly well established.

Other schools were run by churches. As well as providing Sunday schools they began to open more and more day schools. Often, there was a teacher and over a hundred pupils in one large room. It was hard to keep order; bad behaviour was punished severely, and many children were caned until they bled. Older pupils, called monitors, did a lot of the teaching. They stayed behind after school for extra lessons. Then, the next day, they taught small groups of younger pupils.

Some schools were very poor indeed. A government inspector said that at one school:

The children were playing in the open yard, and the master was ... sawing up the blackboard. His books and materials for teaching ... consisted of six Bibles, some copy books, one slate, half a dozen loose and ragged leaves of Reading Made Easy and the remains of the blackboard ... supported on either side by a hand-saw and a hammer.

Queen Victoria's government wanted every child to go to school, and they also wanted to make schools better and less overcrowded. In 1870 they told local councils to set up their own schools if extra places were needed. Then, in 1876, a new law said that children must go to school until they were twelve or thirteen.

? Ragged schools

Think about what you have read about schools.

1. How do you think 'ragged schools' got their name? Do you think children had to pay to attend them? Why?
2. The man who founded the ragged school did not mention teaching the children to read or teaching them about the Bible.
   What did he seem to care about most?
3. Why do you think the teacher was sawing up his blackboard? Find out why teachers and pupils used slates in Victorian schools.
4. In 1842 a teenage boy said:
   "I cannot read much ... I have read the spelling book and Ready-ma-deasy. I cannot write."
   What do you think he meant by Ready-ma-deasy?
   (Read this page again if you need a clue.)
   What does his mistake tell us?
5. Look at the photographs. How were Victorian classrooms different from yours?

1882
May 26

Another case of the
same sort as last
week happened
again last Monday
- a woman using
insulting language
in the presence of all the children.
The affair arose from her boy's being
sent home for his schoolmoney.
The case was reported to the Clerk, &
on Wed. night the Board decided to
take such measures as would put a
stop to all such conduct.
The woman has been threatened with
Law if the like occurs again.
Broke up to-day for Whitsuntide.

In Victorian times, the teacher in charge of each school had to keep a 'log' (a sort of diary listing the main events). These extracts are from the log that was kept at Eldwick School, in Bingley, West Yorkshire. (One entry is given in modern printing as well as in the Victorian writing.)

School logs

Study the three pages from the school log.

1. What made the mother angry?
2. What do you think 'schoolmoney' was?
3. John Nutter belonged to the Board (or Committee) which ran the school.
   Why do you think he came 'without notice'?
4. Some teachers still choose monitors to help with jobs. Why would it cause more problems if a monitor was away in Victorian times?

5. Look at the third page from the school log.
   What do you think an 'Object Lesson' was?
   What do you think the initials mean?
   Whose initials do you think they are?
6. How does the children's schooling seem to differ from yours? (You can discuss this and then make a list of points.)
7. Imagine you are a pupil at Eldwick School in the 1880s and write a 'log' or diary from your own point of view. You can write about some of the days in the real log. For example, what was it like for you when the angry mother arrived?

A blazing arch of lucid
glass
Leaps like a fountain
from the grass
To meet the sun.

15. Public Buildings

The Victorians were proud of their towns and cities, and they showed their pride by building magnificent town halls and libraries, many of which are still in use. They were also proud of their success in business, and we still use some of the market halls and corn and cloth exchanges they built.

Northampton Town Hall.

Near to their towns the Victorians built sewage and water works so that people could have clean streets and clean water. At Papplewick near Nottingham the water works had steam-driven pumps to send the water to people's homes. The pumps can still be seen inside the very fine Victorian building. The Victorians showed how important they thought clean water was by decorating the inside with all sorts of water and wild life designs.

Papplewick Pumping Station near Mansfield.

How are they different?

The photographs on these pages show Victorian buildings.

1. How are they different from modern buildings?

Houses of Parliament.

Liverpool Street Station.

Crystal Palace, 1851.

Companies sometimes wanted people to lend them money, perhaps to buy new stock or new ships. They knew that people would only do this if the company seemed to be doing well, so they showed their wealth by spending as much as they could on their buildings. Railway companies were especially keen to attract new investors, and some of their stations look like palaces!

Victorian buildings

Think about the buildings in a town near you.

1. Try to decide if any large buildings in your area look Victorian, then check their dates.
2. Make a list of some large Victorian buildings you know about, including ones you have seen in this book and ones in your area. If you like you can add a note to say what the building tells you about the Victorians. Your own ideas are best but here are two examples:
Saltaire Church - workers were expected to go to church every Sunday;
St Pancras Station - more and more railways were being built.

The Victorians built real palaces too. One of these is the Palace of Westminster, also called the Houses of Parliament. This has lots of towers and spikes, but the Victorians found out how to use metal to make archways and domes. Victorian stations have large arches, and the Albert Hall in London has an enormous dome.

? Public buildings

Look carefully at these pages.

1. What do you think was done in corn and cloth exchanges?
2. Nowadays we rarely think about water and sewage works. Why did the Victorians care about them so much?
3. Why were the Victorians able to build huge archways and domes? Where can we see huge archways which the Victorians built?

St Pancras.

It was not possible to cross the road without having to wade ankle deep in mud or water.

16. Streets and Shopping

Some people had one of these just outside their door. What do you think it was for? Why did they need it?

Muddy streets made shopping hard, especially for women in their long skirts. The Victorians solved the problem of mud by making more and more of their roads from pebbles or blocks of stone. However, shopping could still be dirty and difficult. By the 1870s most new houses had proper toilets but there were more and more horses fouling the streets. Cart-wheels sent filth everywhere, and the noise they made was deafening.

This is how Dickens described a morning scene in a London street:

Now and then a stage coach covered with mud rattled briskly by ... The public houses, with gas-lights burning inside, were already open ... Then came ... groups of labourers going to their work, then men and women with fish-baskets on their heads, donkey carts laden with vegetables, carts filled with livestock or ... meat, and milk-women with pails ... It was market morning. The ground was covered nearly ankle deep with filth ... , and a thick steam ... rising from ... the bodies of the cattle mixed with the fog, which seemed to rest upon the chimney tops ...

Victorian shops

The painting on the left was done in 1898, twenty eight years after Charles Dickens' death.

1. Why do you think it differs so much from Dickens' description? (Try to think of more than one reason.)
2. Why do you think Victorian shops had signs as well as their names in words?
3. What sorts of places still have signs today?
4. Look at the passage by Charles Dickens. Why are there cattle, horses and donkeys in the streets?
5. Dickens mentions fog and chimneys. How do you think the two were connected?
6. Some of the traders went to market but others went from house-to-house. Which people do you think they were? (Hint: we still have the same thing delivered today.)

Victorian shopping at its best.

Shopping

Look at the picture above.

1. What kinds of toys are the shops selling?
2. Why would shopping be pleasant in this place?
3. What type of people could shop there?
4. Why do you think this picture was painted?

Shops were usually small, gloomy rooms in the owner's home. The photograph shows a museum reconstruction of a grocer's shop. Most of the goods were in tubs or sacks, and the grocer used his scales to weigh what each customer wanted. Butter and sugar were in huge blocks; the grocer cut and shaped each customer's piece of butter with two wooden 'patters'; he sold the sugar in lumps which the customer had to break up.

Chemists' shops had shelves full of strange-looking packets and bottles. Often, the chemist had mixed these medicines up himself, using plants and chemicals. He put Latin names on the labels to make the medicines seem special. He also put big pointed bottles of coloured water in his windows. They helped to show which shop it was and they made it look strange and mysterious.

 The chemist

Look at the photograph of the chemist.

1. What is the chemist doing?
2. Why do you think the chemist is dressed this way?
3. How is medicine stored?
4. Can you think of reasons why people would visit the chemist?
5. Is this a real Victorian chemist shop? Give reasons for your answers.

 The grocer

Look at the photograph of the grocer's shop.

1. How do you know this is not a real Victorian shop?
2. Make a list of the goods this shop sells. Tick those goods which are still sold today.
3. Museums often reconstruct the past by building shops and homes as they were in the past. How does this help us understand the past?
4. How could you find out if Victorian shops were really like this?

5. Make a chart which lists the similarities and differences between this Victorian shop and today. You could record it like this:

Victorian and Today Grocers	
Same	Different
People bought coffee	Weighed in Victorian days. In jars and packets today.

> The churches got us to their evening meetings by giving us food. One church gave us potatoes and another gave us buns. We used to dash from church to church grabbing all we could.

17. Food and Drink

What people ate depended on how well paid they were, and this was linked to the job they did.

 In his famous Report, Chadwick gives us clues to the diet of different workers:

The weaver lives on very innutritious poor food, seldom eats meat;
Irishmen subsist chiefly on potatoes;
The collier [coal-miner] ... drinks too much ... and both he and his family partake of animal food every day.

The mill worker has tea, sugar, bread and butter night and morning; meat, and either bread or potatoes, with a pint of beer every day for his dinner.

Traders known as hucksters sold 'tea, coffee, sugar, butter, cheese, bacon ... and other articles to the working people in small quantities'. They charged a very high price and said that this was to make up for people failing to pay their bills. Some traders cheated the poor by selling them food that was stale. For example, they smeared fresh blood over meat that was going bad.

The Victorians had some clever ways of studying what different groups of people ate. For example, they found out the weight of cattle that were driven to a market, then they found out how many people lived in the area. In Manchester, there was enough fresh meat for everyone to have a helping each day. However, the meat was not shared fairly: most of it went to the better-paid workers; the poorer ones had to make do with salted meat like bacon.

Even when parents had enough money they sometimes fed their children badly, since they did not know which foods were best. Doctors complained that children were being given 'bacon, fried meat and fatty potatoes when they had not, perhaps, two teeth in each jaw'. Parents also gave them drugs to send them to sleep; and some parents made themselves drunk in the evenings to forget their hard lives.

Diets improved as trains brought more and more fresh food into city centres. For example, Londoners started to eat Yorkshire rhubarb, and milk reached cities all over the country.

Victorian diet

Read the extracts from Robert Chadwick's report and the child's diary.

1. Write a shopping list for each of the following:
   - a mill worker
   - a maid shopping for a well off family.
2. How did traders cheat people?
3. What kind of shop is it?
4. How many people work there?
5. Why do you think the photograph was taken?
6. Make a list of the products you can see for sale.

Well off people had meat, but this did not always keep them healthy. A Victorian child wrote in her diary:

At dinner time Papa gave Emily a choice piece of pheasant [wild bird] with bread sauce and potato, but she refused the pheasant... so Papa took it to dear Leo ... It was the last thing he ate that he enjoyed.

Victorian cooking

Look at the picture of the cooking range.

1. How do you think the ovens were heated?
2. Where would bread have been baked?
3. How might meat have been cooked?
4. What do you think the chains and pulleys were used for?

To spend an afternoon at the Winter Fair was like a visit to fairyland.

18.
Pleasures and Pastimes

Children usually played in the streets, but for some who were free on a Saturday there was football on a local pitch.

Travelling shows were very popular. There were jugglers, fire-eaters and men with monkeys and dancing bears. There were also Punch and Judy shows in towns and on beaches.

People who went by train to the seaside often took a dip in the water. Men sometimes swam completely naked, but women changed in bathing machines. A bathing machine was a hut on wheels, and the woman could be wheeled right into the water to bathe in private.

At the seaside

Look at the photograph of the beach.

1. What time of year do you think it is?
2. What is the weather like?
3. Why are people using umbrellas?
4. How were the bathing machines moved in and out of the water?
5. List the activities people might do when visiting the seaside for a day.

Children played with simple toys like marbles, skipping ropes or tops.

Balls were too expensive to buy but sometimes they could make their own. One child explained:

In November came pig-killing time. Soon our ears would be tormented with the screams of the expiring [dying] pig; ... we hung round waiting for the bladder, which ... we blew up with a clay pipe stem.

Victorian games

Read these pages and look carefully at the pictures.

1. Use your own words to explain how some children made balls. Do you think you would find this sort of ball in a house like the one in the photograph? Why?
2. Is this a photograph of a 'real' Victorian room? How do you know?
3. How old does the teddy look? Do you think it belongs to the child in the photograph? Give a reason for your answer.

Pleasures and activities

Look at the photographs and read the extracts.

1. Make a list of all the toys and activities, putting one on each line. Now put a tick by any which we still have today, a cross by any we do not have, or a comment to say how things have changed. Perhaps your list will begin like this:

Toy or activity	Comment
Playing football	Victorian children sometimes made their own balls
Watching shows in the street	

2. How well off were the girls who went to the toy fair compared with other Victorian children? Why do you think so?

To spend an afternoon at the Winter Fair ... was like a visit to fairyland, because ... they entered from the gloomy street into a brightly gaslit interior... A brass band played lively marches, and the air was filled with a strong smell of wax dolls ... The smallest room ... contained toys ... for a penny. Whatever money came the girls' way during the year had to be saved for a spree in this room.

Index